# LET'S-A GO!

Published in 2019 by Carlton Books Limited, an imprint of the
Carlton Publishing Group, 20 Mortimer Street, London W1T3JW

Text and design © Carlton Books Limited 2019

A catalogue record for this book is available from the British
Library.

ISBN: 978 1 78739 220 5

Printed in Dubai

10 9 8 7 6 5 4 3

Designed and packaged by: Dynamo Limited
Special Consultant: Max Gold
Written by: Jon Hamblin

# WE LOVE MARIO!

## JON HAMBLIN

# ...TENTS

...ked our top 21 Mario games,
... down from 21 to the best yet! Go
... them out!

# WE LOVE MARIO!

Whether it's his courageous determination to rescue damsels in distress, his love of meatballs or just that moustache, fans can't get enough of Mario. From his first appearance in *Donkey Kong* (1981), through to his recent *Odyssey*, every game offers something different, from an improved way to play to a fresh graphical look, or even a whole new dimension. This freshness makes every Mario game a joy to play.

This is a celebration of the world's favourite plumber – it covers his best games, visits his friends and even offers up a few secrets. See his greatest hits, his weirdest spin-offs and even games that he'd probably rather forget. Jump down the green pipe, and come on a trip to the Mushroom Kingdom!

# IT'S-A MARIO!

| | | BIO: |
|---|---|---|
| FIRST APPEARANCE: DONKEY KONG | | After getting swept down a pipe into the Mushroom Kingdom, Mario vows to protect it against evil. His favourite food? It's-a me-atballs! |
| DEBUT YEAR: | 1981 | |
| APPEARANCES: | 234 | |
| STRENGTH: | 84 | |
| SPEED: | 77 | |
| WISDOM: | 72 | |
| COURAGE: | 89 | |

# #21

# SUPER MARIO BROS.

**The game that started it all – the original *Super Mario Bros.* on the Nintendo Entertainment System. Retro-tastic!**

*Super Mario Bros.* might not have been the first game to feature Mario (that honour belonged to *Donkey Kong* back in 1981), but it was the first game to feature all the elements now associated with everyone's favourite Italian-American plumber. Coins, Goombas, princesses and transforming mushrooms all featured here for the very first time – not to mention Mario's arch-nemesis Bowser.

## PLUMB CRAZY

Each level sees you running from one end to the other, avoiding enemies, grabbing coins and storming castles, as you try to rescue the kidnapped Princess Toadstool. Mushrooms turn you into Super Mario and fire flowers let you shoot fireballs.

## BACK TO BASICS

As a template for the Mario games that were to come, *Super Mario Bros.* changed games forever, but today its gameplay seems a little bit basic. It's fun if you want to see where Mario mania began, but don't expect fireworks. Well, apart from the ones that sometimes appear at the end of a level. (See page 9 for more info!)

### STATS

Released: 1985
Original platform: Nintendo Entertainment System (NES)
Difficulty:
★★★☆☆

MARIO 057700 ⬤×03 WORLD 2-1 TIME 000
5000

# SECRET

Want to know how to get the fireworks at the end of a level? Hit the end level flag when the last digit of the timer displays 1, 3 or 6!

# TRIVIA

*Super Mario Bros.* sold over 40 million copies and was the most successful selling game for three decades! It was eventually knocked off its perch by *Wii Sports* – another Nintendo game!

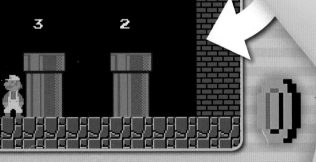

COME TO WARP ZONE!

3        2

# TOP TIP!

When you reach the end of World 1-2, ride the last elevator up to the top and then jump up on to the wall on your right. Run to the end of the level to find pipes that will warp you to higher levels!

# OH, BROTHER!

Luigi hasn't played the hero much since he first appeared in *Mario Bros.* (1983). Even Yoshi has been in more games! Let's take a look at some of them (OK, all of them!) now.

## MARIO IS MISSING!

This educational game for the NES sees Luigi hunting all over the world for his brother. There is no platforming action in this puzzle-based game. Instead Luigi visits each location (including Paris, London and New York), where he must talk to the locals to find out which landmark is missing, and then defeat a Koopa Trooper to restore it to its rightful place. Not great if you want some fun, but good if you need to brush up on your geography. Maybe Mario is right to sit this one out!

### STATS

Released: 1994
Original Platform:
NES
Difficulty:

⭐☆☆☆☆

## IT'S-A LUIGI!

| FIRST APPEARANCE: | | BIO: Luigi goes |
|---|---|---|
| MARIO BROS. | | to the Mushroom |
| DEBUT YEAR: | 1983 | Kingdom, where |
| APPEARANCES: | 181 | he keeps bragging |
| STRENGTH: | 76 | about how much |
| SPEED: | 82 | bigger his mansion |
| WISDOM: | 64 | is than Mario's |
| COURAGE: | 43 | humble toadstool. |

# LUIGI'S MANSION

After winning a competition that he didn't enter, Luigi takes Mario to check out his prize (a mansion!) only to discover that it is actually a rotting shell filled with ghosts called Boos. To make things worse, Mario goes missing again! Luckily, Luigi has the Poltergust 3000, a powerful vacuum gun that can suck up ghosts. Can Luigi rid the house of Boos and find his brother? With its fantastic graphics and original gameplay, Luigi's Mansion is a great ghostbusting simulator, and easily one of the best Mario spin-off games – but not one for those of a nervous disposition!

## STATS
Released: 2001
Original Platform: GameCube
Difficulty:
⭐⭐⭐☆☆

# NEW SUPER LUIGI U

In 2013, Luigi finally got his dues when Nintendo announced his 30th birthday and the start of 'The Year of Luigi'. Loads of Luigi-related merchandise and games were released. These included *Luigi's Mansion: Dark Moon* (a sequel to *Luigi's Mansion* for the 3DS), *Dr. Luigi* (a Dr. Mario-style puzzle game) and Luigi's greatest gaming achievement to date: *New Super Luigi U*. Originally released as add-on levels for *New Super Mario Bros. U* (2012), *New Super Luigi U* was eventually released as a stand-alone title, too. Featuring all the platforming action you'd expect from a Mario title, with the added bonus that Luigi can run slightly faster and jump slightly higher, this game truly puts you through your paces. If you want to see what Mario's younger brother is really capable of, then check this one out.

## STATS
Released: 2013
Original Platform: Wii U
Difficulty:
⭐⭐⭐⭐☆

# #20

# SUPER MARIO BROS. 2

The odd one out in the numbered *Super Mario Bros.* games, *Super Mario Bros. 2* definitely is a strange game.

This game takes place in the world of Subcon instead of the usual Mushroom Kingdom, and while some of the characters are recognizable, others are unique to this title, and they never appear again. *Super Mario Bros. 2* doesn't really play like a Mario game – you can't stomp on enemies' heads, instead you have to resort to throwing vegetables at them. Well, it's one way to get your five-a-day!

## STATS

Released: 1988
Original Platform: NES
Difficulty:
★★★★☆

## UNIQUE SKILLS

One thing that the game did introduce was different abilities for each of the four playable characters, like high jumps for Luigi and long, floating jumps for Princess Peach. These moves later appeared in games like *Super Mario 3D World*. It's also interesting for being one of the few games where the Princess doesn't get captured by Bowser – it turns out it was all just a Mario dream!

## TRIVIA

*Super Mario Bros. 2* started out as *Yume Kōjō: Doki Doki Panic*. Nintendo wanted a sequel to the super successful *Super Mario Bros.* fast, so they just changed the name and the main characters to Mario characters, which may explain why it's so different from the other *Super Mario Bros.* games!

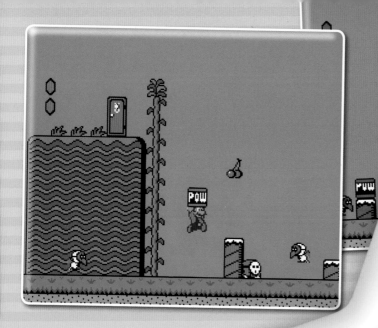

## TOP TIP!

Use coins to win extra lives in the slot machine at the end of each level. To get more coins on Level 1-2, place a potion next to the exit of the underground level. Enter Sub-Space, grab six coins, then run right to fall out of the level. You'll reappear next to the exit door, and you can repeat the trick as many times as you like!

## SECRET

Super Mario Bros. 2 features a cheat code – unfortunately all it does is kill your character! Still, if you want to give it a go, pause the game, then hold UP, B and A on controller two and then unpause.

# OCCUPATIONAL HAZARDS

Although he's best known for plumbing, Mario's CV is stacked with interesting jobs. Over the years he's done everything from practising medicine to becoming a sports star.

## DOCTOR

**What he did:** In *Doctor Mario*, our hero donned a white coat and started helping the residents of the Mushroom Kingdom in a different way – by curing their illnesses. Doctor Mario fought viruses by lobbing mega vitamins at them in this tricky falling block puzzle game. *Doctor Mario* first appeared on the NES, but returned most recently in *Doctor Mario: Miracle Cure* (2015) on the 3DS.

**Was he any good?** The Doctor is IN! Doctor Mario cured many people over the years, including Bowser, who caught a bad case of the Blorbs in *Mario & Luigi: Bowser's Inside Story* (2009).

### STATS
First Appearance: *Doctor Mario*
Year: 1990
Star rating:
★★★☆☆

## RACING DRIVER

**What he did:** Mario has always had a need for speed, so it's no surprise that he's a demon on the kart track, too. He first began his racing history in 1992, when he and his pals raced in the first Mushroom Cup. He's subsequently beaten everyone from Donkey Kong to Yoshi to pole position, and if his recent appearance in *Mario Kart 8 Deluxe* (2017) is anything to go by, he'll be bringing home the trophies for many years to come.

**Was he any good?** He may not be the fastest racer but he's quick off the starting line, and his power slide boost is still one of the coolest moves on the track.

### STATS
First Appearance: *Super Mario Kart*
Year: 1992
Star rating:
★★★★☆

# BUILDER

**What he did:** With his background in carpentry and plumbing, Mario has always been a dab hand when it comes to handyman work, so it was no surprise when he took on the role of builder in *Super Mario Maker* in 2015. Mario understood the construction process perfectly, teaching people how to construct their dream levels. In fact, the only aspect of being a builder he got wrong, was actually turning up when he said he would…

**Was he any good?** Mario helped millions of fans build their own Mario levels, so we'd say he was pretty successful. Although we can't imagine many people were impressed when they moved into their new houses, only to find them stuffed full of Thwomps and Goombas.

## STATS

First Appearance:
*Super Mario Maker*
Year: 2015
Star rating:

★★★☆☆

# TENNIS PLAYER

**What he did:** Mario's first court appearance was in *Mario's Tennis* (1995), a 3D tennis game for the Virtual Boy, an early attempt at a 3D console by Nintendo that failed to gain much popularity. Mario's tennis career was a different story, though. He went on to appear in six more tennis games, including the most recent *Mario Tennis Aces* (2018) on the Nintendo Switch.

**Was he any good?** Mario was the #1 seeded player in the Mushroom Kingdom for a time, until he was knocked off the top spot by Bowser. But Bowser's unsportsmanlike use of a fireball to knock Mario off the winner's podium meant the title was returned to Mario again.

## STATS

First Appearance:
*Mario's Tennis*
Year: 1995
Star rating:

★★★

# BASEBALL PLAYER

**What he did:** After conquering the worlds of racing and tennis, Mario went to bat for the Mario Sunshines, taking on baseball as his next sporting challenge. As a pitcher, he developed his famous fire ball, which saw his baseball explode into flames as it flew towards nervous batters armed only with a very flammable bit of wood.

**Was he any good?** Mario excelled as both a pitcher and a fielder, and his wall jump catch was the talk of the stadium. The baseball season came to an unfortunate end, however, when rabid fans mistook Yoshi for a team mascot, and tried to pull his head off.

## STATS

First Appearance: *Mario Superstar Baseball*
Year: 2005
Star rating:

# PIRATE

**What he did:** Mario decided to give up his landlubber status and embrace a life of piracy when he bought this outfit in the Seaside Kingdom gift shop. We're not quite sure he found his sea legs though, and there are still rumours that he was spotted jumping over the side of his ship into Bubblaine's bay.

**Was he any good?** To be honest, while he wears the costume well, we're not sure Mario is cut-throat enough to be a pirate. Sure he's great at amassing huge piles of gold, but we can't imagine him making anyone walk the plank.

## STATS

First Appearance: *Super Mario Odyssey*
Year: 2017
Star rating:

## ASTRONAUT

**What he did:** No stranger to space exploration after his adventures in the *Super Mario Galaxy* games, Mario finally purchased a spacesuit while exploring the Moon Kingdom in *Super Mario Odyssey* (2017). He also wore it to explore the *Dark Side of the Moon*, the *Darker Side of the Moon*, and to bed most nights!

**Was he any good?** Mario made one small step for an Italian-American plumber, but one giant leap for gaming, bouncing around on the surface of the Moon Kingdom like a pro. Neil Armstrong would be proud.

### STATS
**First Appearance:**
*Super Mario Odyssey*
**Year:** 2017
**Star rating:**
⭐⭐⭐⭐☆

## ARTIST

**What he did:** Tired of spending his days jumping on Goombas and defeating Bowser, in 1992, Mario decided to take up a more relaxing hobby – painting. Unfortunately, back then, computer drawing programs were not very advanced, and so everything Mario tried to create came out blocky. Maybe it's just as well he went back to saving Princess Peach afterwards.

**Was he any good?** Although Mario tried his very best to create awesome artwork, his paintings were not well received by the artistic community. Critics describe Mario's mural masterpiece, 'The Creation of Bob-omb' in harsh terms, calling it "a failed attempt…" and "rubbish." Never mind, Mario, your fans love you!

### STATS
**First Appearance:**
*Mario Paint*
**Year:** 1992
**Star rating:**
⭐☆☆☆☆

# SUPER MARIO BROS. 3

*Super Mario Bros. 3* was the game that made Mario a household name around the world, and it's easy to see why.

The running and jumping in this third game of the *Super Mario Bros.* series is honed to perfection, and there's a meaty selection of levels to test your platforming skills, too. *Super Mario Bros. 3* introduces a lot of the Mario staples – it's the first time you see a world map, and Mario's iconic raccoon suit gets its first airing along with a variety of other fun suits. Also, Bowser introduces his rotten family, the Koopalings, for the first time. Of all the Mario games available on the *NES*, *Super Mario Bros. 3* is the one that's still the most fun to play today.

## TRIVIA

This game featured in the 1989 film, *The Wizard.* In it, two brothers take a road trip to a video game tournament. The final challenge: play a level of *Super Mario Bros. 3*. It went on to become one of the best-selling games of the 90s.

## STATS

Released: 1988
Original Platform:
NES
Difficulty:
★★☆

# TOP TIP!

To get a warp whistle, go to Level 1-3. Near the end of the level, there's a white platform. Stand on it, and hold DOWN for five seconds. Mario will fall down behind the scenery. Run all the way to the right, and you'll enter a secret toad house, where you'll find a warp whistle in a chest. Blow it on the world map to be whisked away to a level select screen!

# SECRET

Mario's creator Shigeru Miyamoto says that *Super Mario Bros. 3* takes place in a theatre. That's why the title screen has an opening curtain, there are catwalks and props in the background, and darkness at the end of each level, or scene!

# YO! YOSHI

From the moment Mario first broke Yoshi out of prison in *Super Mario World*, they've been the best of friends. With his long tongue and amazing egg-throwing skills, Yoshi is more than a match for most enemies. Over the years, Yoshi's had plenty of time in the spotlight. Let's take a look at some of his solo adventures!

## SUPER MARIO WORLD 2: YOSHI'S ISLAND

Although numbered as a sequel to *Super Mario World*, *Yoshi's Island* is, confusingly, the earliest game in Mario's timeline – it features Mario and Luigi as babies. This contradicts the story of Mario and Luigi travelling to the Mushroom Kingdom from New York, but that's probably the nature of legends – who knows which story is really true? At any rate, *Yoshi's Island* has a beautiful hand-crafted pastel art style. The game sees our dinosaur friend looking after Baby Mario as he tracks down Baby Bowser, who has kidnapped Baby Luigi with the help of the magician Kamek. It seems like, even as a child, Bowser was keen on taking things that weren't his! Although the gameplay is very different from other Mario platform games (here, your health is linked to time – after taking

a hit, you only have a few seconds to grab Baby Mario before you lose a life), *Yoshi's Island is* still one of the best.

### STATS

Released: 1995
Original Platform: SNES
Difficulty:
★★★★☆

20

# YOSHI'S TOUCH AND GO

*Yoshi's Touch and Go* is an easy game to fall for – or, at least, it is if you're Baby Mario, who starts each level by being knocked from the beak of a delivery stork by the magician Kamek! It's your job to make Mario's fall to earth as graceful as possible, by drawing lines of clouds on the screen to act as buffers to break Baby Mario's fall.

You can also draw bubbles around enemies to get extra coins. How many coins you get determines what colour Yoshi will be when he catches you. It's a simple game, but it can be quite stressful as your hastily drawn lines push Baby Mario close to spikes and enemies that could end the round. But if you like fun puzzle games, you'll be on cloud nine.

**STATS**
Released: 2005
Original Platform:
Nintendo DS
Difficulty:
⭐⭐⭐☆☆

# YOSHI

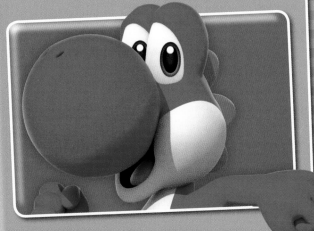

**FIRST APPEARANCE:** SUPER MARIO WORLD

**DEBUT YEAR:** 1990

**APPEARANCES:** 91

**STRENGTH:** 63

**SPEED:** 92

**WISDOM:** 34

**COURAGE:** 67

**BIO:** Yoshi (full name, T. Yoshisaur Munchakoopas) is trapped inside an egg, until Mario cracks it open and the two become firm friends!

# YOSHI'S STORY

**STATS**
Released: 1997
Original Platform:
N64
Difficulty:
⭐⭐⭐☆☆

Finally, it's time for Yoshi to fly solo in his first N64 adventure. Although similar in gameplay to the *Yoshi's Island* games, this is the first Yoshi game to not feature Baby Mario. Instead, Yoshi and his pals are trying to reclaim their Super Happy Tree, which has been stolen by a jealous Baby Bowser. Although the 3D graphics aren't quite as charming as the 2D pastels of *Yoshi's Island*, there's still plenty of dinosaur fun to be had. Yoshi eats, shoots and poops, all while running around with his eggy-entourage!

# YOSHI'S WOOLLY WORLD

## STATS

Released: 2015
Original Platform:
Wii U
Difficulty:

★★☆☆☆

Did you hear about the time Yoshi was made of wool? On this woolly island, Kamek is up to his old tricks again, turning all the Yoshis into bundles of wool.    It's up to Yarn Yoshi to unravel the mystery and restore all his friends to their woolly selves. The game looks gorgeous, with every strand of Yoshi's yarn looking like it was lovingly knitted by hand. Like knitting, this game isn't very difficult to pick up, but you'll still get needled if you pick the more tricky routes through the game.

# YOSHI'S SAFARI

In the early 90s, plastic guns were all the rage when it came to video games. Games like *Lethal Enforcers* and *Virtua Cop* filled the arcades. It was no surprise that Nintendo wanted a piece of the action – but it was a bit surprising that they picked Yoshi as their gunslinging hero. *Yoshi's Safari* was an on-rails, shooting gallery game, designed to be used with the Super Scope Light Gun. The game sees you in Mario's shoes (the only time Nintendo has ever produced a through-Mario's-eyes perspective game to date), blasting away at waves of flying Koopa Troopas as you try to rescue King Fret of Jewellery Land. Seeing the Koopalings and Bowser re-imagined as giant mechs is certainly interesting, but it's perhaps unsurprising that Mario took a break from guns for a couple of decades after this.

## STATS

Released: 1995
Original Platform:
SNES
Difficulty:

★★☆

## YOSHI'S COOKIE

Everyone knows how much Yoshi loves food, so it's inevitable that he has an entire game set in a cookie factory. In *Yoshi's Cookie*, Mario and Yoshi spend all day making cookies. As the cookies drop from the top and roll in from the right of the screen, it's your job to make them disappear. No, not into your tummy! It's a fun puzzle game, and for the *SNES* version, the puzzles were designed by Alexey Pajitnov, the genius creator of the original Tetris game. This tasty game is definitely one to get!

### STATS
Released: 1992
Original Platform: NES
Difficulty:
★★★★☆

The most recent game in the *Yoshi's Island* series (despite not actually featuring the island), sees Kamek once again trying to steal the Mario Babies as Baby Mario and Yoshi must try to rescue Baby Luigi. This time, Yoshi can create massive eggs called Mega Eggdozers. While producing these must cause quite a strain on his insides, the results are incredibly useful, as these bad boy eggs can destroy everything in their path. Eggs-plosive gameplay aside, this is not the most imaginative game in the *Yoshi's Island* series, and the choice of a kazoo for the soundtrack will have you pressing the mute button long before the game is over.

### STATS
Released: 2014
Original Platform: 3DS
Difficulty:
★★★☆

# #18

# SUPER MARIO WORLD

Yes, it's Yoshi time! *Super Mario World* really is the highest point in the awesomely timeless 2D Super Mario adventures.

Now we're talking – it's Yoshi time! *Super Mario World* was the pinnacle of the 2D Mario adventures. It featured brilliantly colourful graphics (thanks to the enhanced power of the SNES) and a massive 96 levels, many of which were hidden. Found in an egg while the Mario Brothers were holidaying on Dinosaur Island, Yoshi goes on to become one of Mario's most constant companions, appearing in some form or another in almost every Mario game ever since.

## STATS

Released: 1990
Original Platform: SNES
Difficulty:
★★★★☆

## IT'S A MYSTERY

This game is stuffed full of twisty secrets, involving hidden exits, secret levels, and even secret worlds. Uncovering all of its mysteries by yourself could take years. It is definitely time well spent – but remember to take regular breaks!

## ? TRIVIA

Game critics loved *Super Mario World*, giving it top marks when it was released. In 2009, *Empire* magazine readers even voted it the greatest game of all time.

## TOP TIP!

Reach the Star Road and you can find and hatch different-coloured Yoshi eggs. Baby Yoshis become adult Yoshis with one power up, five berries or five baddies. Each Yoshi has a special skill if he eats Koopa shells of the same colour. Blue Yoshis fly, Red Yoshis spit fire and Yellow Yoshis do mega stomps!

## SECRET

Yoshi was originally designed for another game, *Devil World*. When a dinosaur theme was picked for *Super Mario World*, Mario creator Shigeru Miyamoto updated his first sketch to create Yoshi!

# #17

# SUPER MARIO 64

**After more than a decade of running left to right (and right to left), *Super Mario 64* took Mario to a new dimension – the third one!**

In 1996, Mario finally made the leap to 3D, defying critics who said it couldn't be done. *Super Mario 64* was incredible for a number of reasons. It was one of the first fully 3D platform games – not the very first though, *Alpha Waves* (1990) on the Atari ST home computer has that honour. It was a free-roaming, open world game and it looked beautiful. More importantly, *Super Mario 64* played beautifully, too. In addition to adding many of the acrobatic moves Mario is now famous for, it also set the standard for how to best show action in 3D games, featuring a game camera that rarely needed to be moved and never got in your way.

## RESCUE MISSION

When it comes to the story, *Super Mario 64* is on more familiar ground. Princess Peach invites Mario to her castle for a slice of cake and she gets kidnapped by Bowser AGAIN. Mario gets to jump through paintings in the castle to visit various levels where he can collect the stars he needs to defeat Bowser and rescue Princess Peach.

## LEADER OF THE PACK

*Super Mario 64* had a huge impact on gamers and gaming when it was released. Seeing the world's favourite plumber run around the Mushroom Kingdom in all three dimensions for the first time truly was a breathtaking sight. This is one of the most iconic Mario games, and it provided the template for all 3D Mario games to come.

## STATS

Released: 1996
Original Platform: N64
Difficulty:

★★☆

## TRIVIA

Opening with, "It's-a me, Mario!" *Super Mario 64* was the first time most gamers heard Mario speak. Charles Martinet was the man responsible for giving Mario a voice.

## TOP TIP!

Get infinite lives outside the castle at the start of the game. First climb the third tree from the waterfall to grab an extra life. Then, whenever you come out of the castle, this extra life will return – every time!

## SECRET

Although not in the main game, Yoshi does make an appearance in *Super Mario 64*! If you manage to get all 120 stars, a cannon next to the river outside the castle starts working! Use it to get up onto the roof of Peach's castle where Yoshi is waiting to congratulate you with 100 lives!

# #16

# SUPER MARIO SUNSHINE

**Mario's tropical adventure wasn't his best ever, but it certainly made a splash…**

Everyone needs a holiday every now and then, and Mario is no exception. In *Super Mario Sunshine*, our plucky plumber heads off to the tropical paradise of Isle Delfino for some well earned rest and relaxation. Except, of course, everything goes wrong almost as soon as his plane's wheels touch the tarmac. Mario gets framed for covering the entire island in graffiti. Princess Peach gets kidnapped by the true vandal, a dark double known as Shadow Mario. There's nothing for Mario to do but clean up the city and rescue Princess Peach.

## SHORE THING

With its famously flaky camera, *Super Mario Sunshine* wasn't as polished as some of the other games in the *Super Mario* series. But this doesn't stop it from being brilliantly unique with its vertical platforming and its focus on… community service! A great place to go on holiday but you may not want to live there.

## SPRAY TIME

Luckily, Mario's armed with more than just a bucket of soapy water and a sponge! Professor Elvin Gadd has given our hero a F.L.U.D.D. (which stands for Flash Liquidizer Ultra Dousing Device, apparently) backpack. This is a portable fire hose that lets Mario spray water, fight enemies and even hover in the air!

### STATS

Released: 2002
Original Platform: GameCube
Difficulty:
★★★☆☆

# TOP TIP!

Need some lives fast? If you return to Pianta Village and replay Episode 6: Piantas in Need, the villagers will give you 1-ups instead of blue coins when you save all the Piantas!

# SECRET

Once you've collected 30 Shines, find the man wearing shades in Delfino Plaza. He'll give you a pair! Talk to him again after you've won the game for this Hawaiian shirt, too!

# TRIVIA

F.L.U.D.D. inventor, Professor Elvin Gadd, is the James Dyson of the Mario world, a vacuum obsessive who also created the Poltergust 3000 in *Luigi's Mansion*.

# FAMILY VALUES

Despite his bad boy image, many people forget that Bowser is also a single parent, struggling to raise eight unruly kids – although he disagrees that most of the Koopalings belong to him, insisting that Bowser Jr. is his only true son. Here's an in-depth look at his whole rotten family tree.

As the patriarch of the clan, Bowser rules his family with an iron claw. Or at least, he attempts to – his offspring seem to have a habit of getting into plenty of mischief behind his back, stealing magical artefacts, kidnapping princesses and causing trouble. It seems the apple really doesn't fall far from the tree.

## BOWSER

| | |
|---|---|
| **FIRST APPEARANCE:** SUPER MARIO BROS. | **BIO:** Mario's arch nemesis Bowser is the King of the Koopas. Fierce and fond of kidnapping, he does sometimes do the right thing – if it benefits him! |
| **DEBUT YEAR:** 1985 | |
| **APPEARANCES:** 156 | |
| **STRENGTH:** 63 | |
| **SPEED:** 53 | |
| **WISDOM:** 44 | |
| **COURAGE:** 33 | |

## MRS BOWSER

No one knows the identity of the mother of Bowser's children. Bowser himself once told Bowser Jr. that it was Princess Peach, although this later turned out to be a lie. Whoever she is, we're pretty sure she's out of the picture now.

## LARRY

The youngest Koopaling, Larry is notable for his shock of bright blue hair. Being the youngest, he craves attention and often flies into rages when he doesn't get what he wants.

## BOWSER JR.

The oldest of Bowser's children and heir to the Bowser throne, Bowser Jr. is already knee-deep in the family business, having kidnapped Peach in *Super Mario Sunshine* (2003), and attempting to take over the Mushroom Kingdom in *Mario + Rabbids: Kingdom Battle* (2017). A keen petrolhead, he's rarely seen outside his Koopa Clown Car.

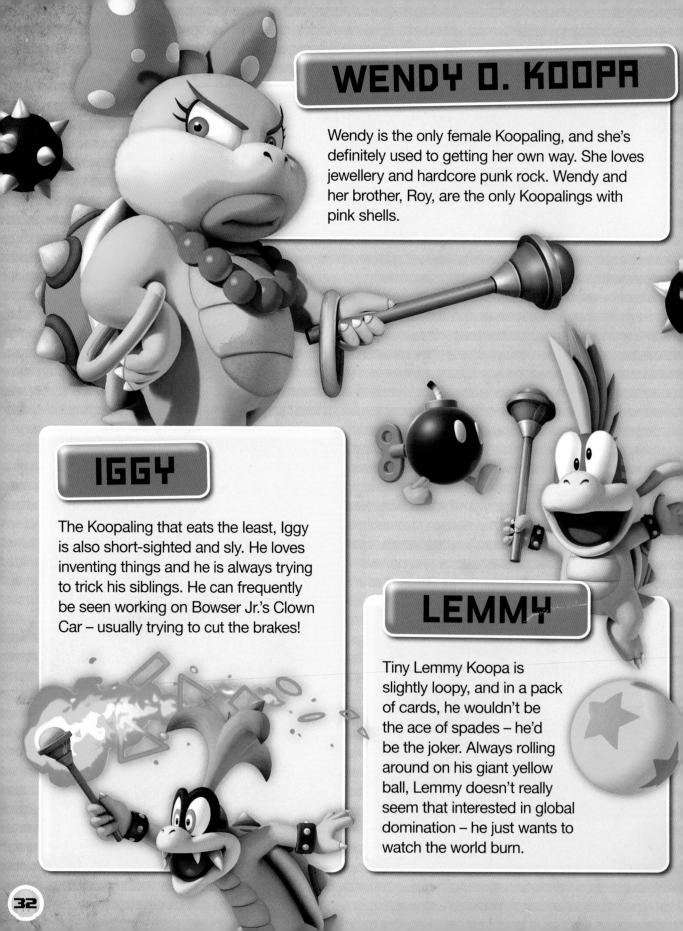

# WENDY O. KOOPA

Wendy is the only female Koopaling, and she's definitely used to getting her own way. She loves jewellery and hardcore punk rock. Wendy and her brother, Roy, are the only Koopalings with pink shells.

# IGGY

The Koopaling that eats the least, Iggy is also short-sighted and sly. He loves inventing things and he is always trying to trick his siblings. He can frequently be seen working on Bowser Jr.'s Clown Car – usually trying to cut the brakes!

# LEMMY

Tiny Lemmy Koopa is slightly loopy, and in a pack of cards, he wouldn't be the ace of spades – he'd be the joker. Always rolling around on his giant yellow ball, Lemmy doesn't really seem that interested in global domination – he just wants to watch the world burn.

## LUDWIG VON KOOPA

Eldest child, Ludwig, is serious and clever – but he's also a bit of a show off, which usually leads to his downfall. Ludwig often tries to take charge of the Koopalings – much to his siblings' glee-filled mockery.

## ROY

Roy is a Koopa-wrecking machine, a tough turtle who prefers brawn (and preferably, explosions) over brains. He may wear hot pink sunglasses, but don't be fooled – they're so he isn't blinded by the light from his latest kaboom.

## MORTON JR.

If you want to know which Koopaling has the biggest mouth, meet Morton Jr. This little thug is always trying to annoy people with his bragging and boasting. He's also extremely protective of his siblings and always looks out for them in a fight.

# #15

# SUPER MARIO GALAXY

**Space may be the final frontier for mere mortals but for Mario, it's just another day saving Princess Peach.**

This time, Princess Peach has carelessly let her entire castle get kidnapped by Bowser, who has placed it at the centre of the universe. Can you guess whose job it is to rescue her? *Super Mario Galaxy* was the first major Mario game on the Nintendo Wii, and it is epic. There's a powerful, orchestral soundtrack, an intergalactic story spanning a whole galaxy of planets and most importantly, the introduction of Mario's iconic spin attack.

of more traditional Mario power-ups, like Fire Flowers and Ice Flowers, as well as Bee, Boo and Spring Suits, similar to the suits found in *Super Mario Bros. 3* (1988). Most Mario games are great but *Super Mario Galaxy* is out of this world.

## STATS

Released: 2007
Original Platform: Wii
Difficulty:
⭐⭐⭐⭐⭐

## MOON MISSION

Mario must leap through space, jumping from one moon to another as he fights his way ever closer to the centre of the universe. This is the Mario game where everything works like a star-studded dream. The controls feel tight, the action is fluid, and most importantly, almost every few minutes, there is something new to put a smile on your face. It also sees the return

## SECRET

Travel to the Rolling Gizmo galaxy, and instead of jumping on the star ball, run to the still-upright bridge. Jump up on top of it and look down, and you'll be able to see this Rupee-shaped homage to the *Legend of Zelda* series.

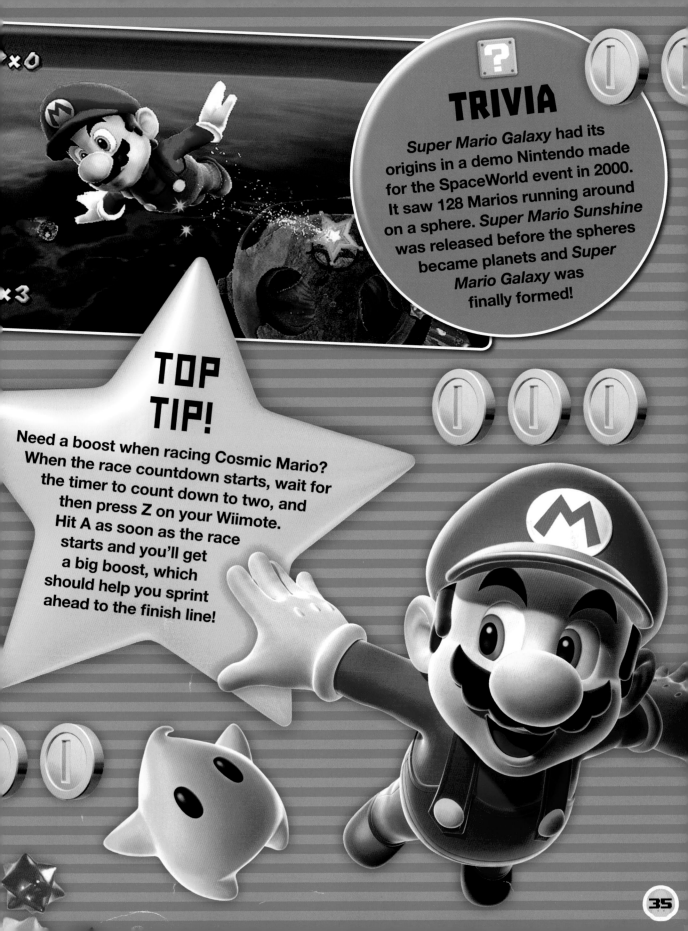

## TRIVIA

*Super Mario Galaxy* had its origins in a demo Nintendo made for the SpaceWorld event in 2000. It saw 128 Marios running around on a sphere. *Super Mario Sunshine* was released before the spheres became planets and *Super Mario Galaxy* was finally formed!

## TOP TIP!

Need a boost when racing Cosmic Mario? When the race countdown starts, wait for the timer to count down to two, and then press Z on your Wiimote. Hit A as soon as the race starts and you'll get a big boost, which should help you sprint ahead to the finish line!

# #14

# SUPER MARIO GALAXY 2

Oh no! Bowser has kidnapped Princess Peach and hidden her at the centre of the universe... again?

If *Super Mario Galaxy 2*'s plot sounds familiar, that's perhaps because it didn't start out as a sequel. Its working title was actually *Super Mario Galaxy More* and it was originally intended to be a quick follow-up offering remixed planets and new challenges. But of course, it didn't work out that way! Once the team started adding new powers and thinking about the return of everyone's favourite green dinosaur, Yoshi, the add-on turned into a full-blown sequel. In interviews, Mario creator Shigeru Miyamoto compared it to *The Legend of Zelda: Majora's Mask* (2000), in that both games used the same game engine as the previous title in the series, but both built massively on those foundations.

## BASICS

This game is definitely harder than the previous one, and certain levels will have you flipping your Wiimote in frustration. But there's platforming gold in these hills, and the addition of Yoshi adds so much to the fun as you slingshot your way around the fun-packed planetoids.

## STATS

Released: 2010
Original Platform: Wii
Difficulty:
★★★★☆

## TRIVIA

Originally, Donkey Kong and Pikmin were going to put in an appearance, but then it was decided that Pikmin simply didn't fit in! Donkey Kong was also dropped but he shows up in a later Mario game.

## TOP TIP!

Travel to the Supermassive Galaxy, race past the Thwomps and fly to the small brown disc with three Koopas on it. Get a friend to use the second Wiimote to freeze a Koopa, and jump on! Keep bouncing on the shell (without touching the ground) to get 1-ups. Then watch your total climb to 99!

## SECRET

Travel to the Shiverburn Galaxy, look up at the mountains and you'll see three shadowy figures. Who are they? You decide!

# THE PRINCESS DIARIES

Princess Peach has been friends with Mario since the very beginning, but what does she really think of him? Well, here's what we think Peach's diary entries might be like!

## PRINCESS PEACH

**FIRST APPEARANCE:** SUPER MARIO BROS.

**DEBUT YEAR:** 1985

**APPEARANCES:** 169

**STRENGTH:** 52

**SPEED:** 81

**WISDOM:** 88

**COURAGE:** 97

**BIO:** The leader of the Mushroom Kingdom is classy, graceful, and obsessed with the colour pink. She also gets kidnapped A LOT!

## Tuesday 3rd September, 1985

11 am: So far, today has been absolutely awful. The whole castle — myself included — woke up late after last night's Star Festival. My feet are so sore! Why are princesses made to wear such silly high-heeled shoes? They are impossible to walk in, never mind dance in!

When I went to find Toad to ask him for a foot rub, Bowser was banging at the castle door. I knew I shouldn't have answered it but I've been brought up to be polite to everyone, even villains, so I found myself letting him in. Before I knew it, he had tucked me under his arm and was carrying me off to one of his nasty castles. This dungeon is extremely dark, damp and cold... but I will find a way to escape!

1 pm: The dungeon door broke open to reveal Mario! He assured me Bowser was defeated and took me back to my castle. He is such a brave and true friend. And he always turns up in my darkest hour

to provide help. I really do not know what I would do without him. Perhaps I should make him a lord... or maybe a knight?

## Monday 5th May, 2002

7 am: I threw open the doors of my apartment to reveal an amazing view of Delfino Plaza, and beyond that, the sea, sparkling in the sun like a million glittering jewels. Even princesses deserve a holiday every now and then! I'm really looking forward to heading down to the beach, feeling the sand between my toes and forgetting my responsibilities for a while. Is that bad of me? I honestly do love my job and my loyal subjects!

7 pm: I have been kidnapped again. This really is getting beyond a joke!

## Friday 3rd February, 2007

9 pm: I knew it. I just KNEW it! A kidnapping was — quite literally! — written in the stars today, so I made sure I had a suitcase packed. It turns out I needn't have troubled myself, as Bowser abducted the entire castle this time, and has somehow managed to hide us all at the centre of the universe! At least the stars outside my window are pretty. I can't imagine Mario will be able to come to our rescue this time, though.
11 pm: Mario DID come to our rescue, and

he brought someone called Rosalina with him. Perhaps we could be friends? It can get terribly lonely being a princess — never mind one that is constantly being kidnapped!

## Thursday 17th October, 2017

5pm: Today, Bowser stooped to an all-time low when he tried to force me to marry him. Luckily, just as the ceremony was about to begin, Mario arrived and started jumping on everyone's head, which was extremely funny! It never occurred to me before that a knight in shining armour could also be a joker!

9pm: Back at the hotel. So thankful that Mario saved the day again! I really must talk to him about how all this kidnapping business with Bowser can be prevented from happening ever again!

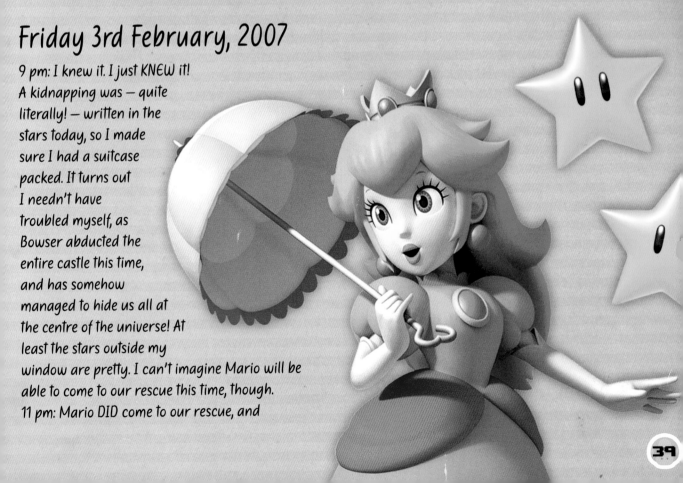

# #13

# SUPER MARIO 3D WORLD

In this Wii U sequel to the popular 3DS game *Super Mario 3D Land* (2011), Nintendo creates something completely new.

This is a mix of the platforming of the original Mario games and the more free-roaming 3D titles. Here the emphasis is on fun platforming, and what's more, you can bring three friends along for some chaotic multi-player gaming.

## PEACH POWER

Of course, being able to pick Princess Peach as a playable character means that this is one of the very few Mario games that DOESN'T feature Peach getting kidnapped by Bowser. He has kidnapped six Sprixie princesses this time though, so he hasn't entirely given up his princess pilfering ways. Will he never stop?

## MULTI-FUN

The multi-player function is a massively exciting new feature in the Mario series, making it feel super fresh!

You haven't lived until you've had a massive argument with your friend about who really deserved the Mushroom pickup that they just swiped from under your nose. If you're up for some playtime with pals, this really is the Mario game for you.

**STATS**

Released: 2013
Original Platform:
Wii U
Difficulty:

⭐⭐☆☆☆

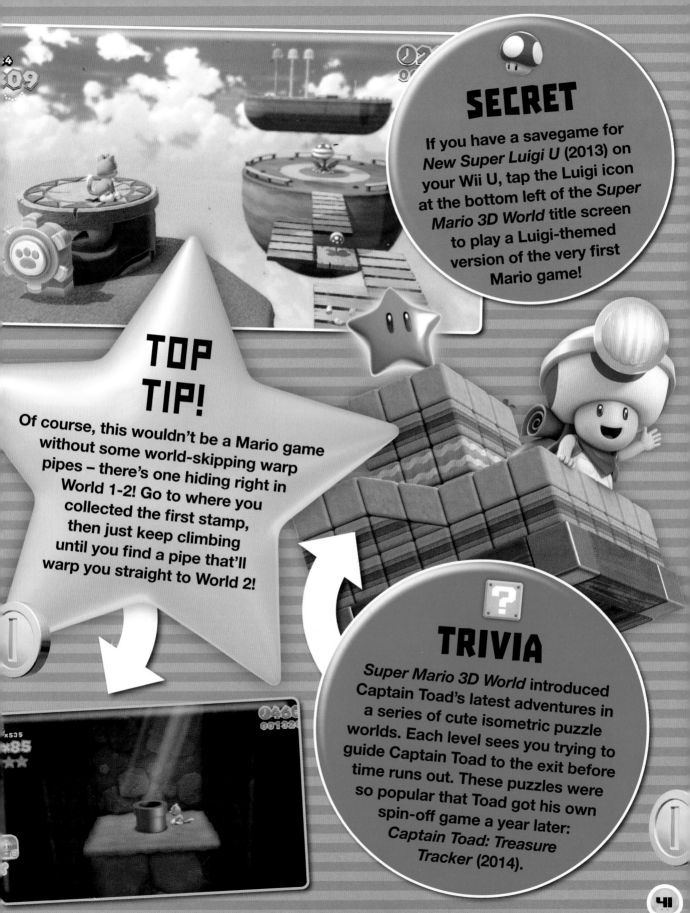

## SECRET

If you have a savegame for *New Super Luigi U* (2013) on your Wii U, tap the Luigi icon at the bottom left of the *Super Mario 3D World* title screen to play a Luigi-themed version of the very first Mario game!

## TOP TIP!

Of course, this wouldn't be a Mario game without some world-skipping warp pipes – there's one hiding right in World 1-2! Go to where you collected the first stamp, then just keep climbing until you find a pipe that'll warp you straight to World 2!

## TRIVIA

*Super Mario 3D World* introduced Captain Toad's latest adventures in a series of cute isometric puzzle worlds. Each level sees you trying to guide Captain Toad to the exit before time runs out. These puzzles were so popular that Toad got his own spin-off game a year later: *Captain Toad: Treasure Tracker* (2014).

# A ROUGH GUIDE TO THE MUSHROOM KINGDOM

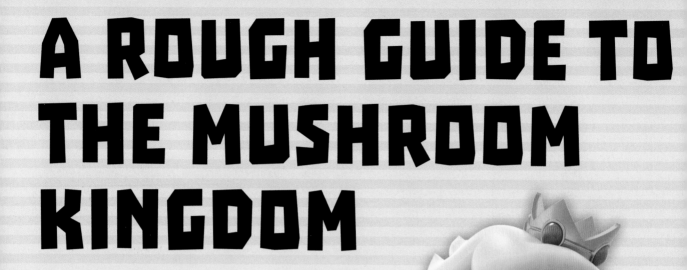

After her ordeal in *Mario Odyssey*, Peach decided to go on holiday. Here are some postcards we think she might have sent while she was away!

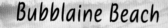

Bubblaine Beach

Dear Toad,
Tiara and I are having a lovely time at Bubblaine Beach. The sand is soft and warm, the sea is crystal clear... We played some volleyball earlier but Tiara kept running away from the ball! Not sure you'd enjoy sunbathing though - it's so popular here, there's not 'mushroom' to lie down! Hehe!

Lots of love, Princess Peach

## New Donk City

Dear Mario,
Wow! You weren't kidding, New Donk City is a bustling place! Found lots of great shops, bought some new hats and even got to see a jazz band. A tour of a large construction site was slightly spoiled by a giant monkey who kept giving me funny looks but otherwise we have had a lovely time. Wish you were here!

Love, Peach x

Dear Toadette,
Tiara insisted we revisit the Moon Cathedral — she loves churches and it really is beautiful! We didn't have much time to enjoy it last time, what with Bowser trying to force me to marry him. I know how much you wanted to be a bridesmaid — I promise that when I CHOOSE to get married, you'll be there by my side.

Kisses, Peach x

## Moon Cathedral

## Peach's Castle

To my loyal subjects,
You may have heard about my kidnapping. I am now safe and I don't imagine Bowser will attempt to snatch me again for a while. Thank you so much for the flowers and kind letters. While I cannot reply to you all personally, I am touched! Looking forward to next week's Star Festival - let's make it the best one ever!

Your loving leader, Princess Peach

# #12

# PAPER MARIO: COLOUR SPLASH

Some Mario fans might agree that the plots in Mario games are paper thin – but in the *Paper Mario* games, they really are!

In a change of pace from the usual platforming action, the *Paper Mario* series introduces role-playing games (or RPGs) to Mario fans, starting with *Super Mario RPG* (1996) on the SNES. This first entry is a more traditional role-playing game, introducing a turn-based combat system to the Mario universe. For the second game in the series, *Paper Mario* (2000), development was handed over to Intelligent Systems, who went on to create all the subsequent *Paper Mario* titles.

elements, while the more recent games, like *Super Paper Mario* (2007), and *Paper Mario: Sticker Star* (2012) featured an emphasis on more exploratory gameplay and fun paper-based mechanics.

## SPLAT-TASTIC!

*Paper Mario: Colour Splash* (2016) is the most recent entry in the series. It sees Paper Mario using his paint hammer to restore colour to Prism Island, after Bowser and his Koopalings have been on a multi-coloured stealing spree. If you want a Mario game that's different from the rest, this one will really let you paint the town red.

## IT'S-A THIN MARIO

In the *Paper Mario* games, Mario is quite literally made out of paper and able to slide, fold and crumple his way into all sorts of small places. The first two games, *Paper Mario* and *Paper Mario: The Thousand Year Door* (2004) both featured quite heavy RPG

## STATS

Released: 2016
Original Platform: Wii U
Difficulty:
★★★★☆

MAX 100

HP 50/50

## TOP TIP!

There's a secret cave behind a large rock at Bloo Bay Beach at the start of the level. Hammer and pull the low hanging vine by the wall to find a huge stash of coins and a Thing card. Quit the level, come back and do it again as many times as you like. Soon you'll have a huge stash of gold coins!

## TRIVIA

Like other *Paper Mario* games, *Colour Splash* loves referencing other Mario titles. Luigi escorts Mario down Rainbow Road in a standard kart – a nod to the legendary racetrack in almost every *Mario Kart* game to date.

## SECRET

In the *Paper Mario* games, you finally get to see where Mario lives. His house has a dining room, a bedroom and a secret basement. Luigi and Mario share a bunk bed – no prizes for guessing which brother gets the top bunk!

# MARIO KART 8 DELUXE

## #11

*Mario Kart* games have appeared on every Nintendo console since the SNES, inspiring many other kart-based racing games!

From *Donkey Kong* to *Sonic*, a whole host of similar racing games followed the turbo-charged success of *Super Mario Kart* (1992). But no one does it better than Mario, and it's easy to see why. *Super Mario Kart* put the series on the starting line, and it's amazing how many of the elements were already in place in that first game. It had a team of Nintendo all-star racers, plenty of power-ups, and a range of sneaky shortcuts for gaining an advantage over your friends. It also featured the 'elastic band' artificial intelligence that lets racers at the back of the pack move faster to ensure that races are always close and exciting.

using their transforming karts to drive up walls and even race upside down! Online races allow for up to 12 players, too, so gameplay is more exciting than ever. But don't show off if you manage to get to first place – a leader-seeking blue koopa shell is never far away...

## GOING UP THE WALL

In *Mario Kart 8 Deluxe* (2017) on Nintendo Switch, Mario and friends can flip gravity as well as the script,

### STATS

Released: 2017
Original Platform:
Nintendo Switch
Difficulty:

⭐⭐⭐☆☆

# TOP TIP!

At the start of any race, wait for the second green light, then hit the accelerate button. If timed correctly, you'll speed to the front of the pack. Practise getting this move right because this tip applies to all *Mario Kart* games!

## TRIVIA

Mario Kart 8 introduced the Luigi Death Stare. Seen whenever Luigi passes players on the track, it has become a viral internet meme!

## SECRET

While driving around Toad Harbour, try to spot a giant statue of Princess Peach out at sea that resembles the Statue of Liberty. Unlike the famous New York icon, this one probably wasn't built by the French.

# MARIO SPORTS SUPERSTARS

**#10**

Over the years Mario has entered everything from golf tournaments to the Olympics. The question is: do you think you can keep up?

*Mario Sports Superstars* attempts to bring five sports – golf, baseball, football, tennis and horse racing – into one game for the first time. Of these five sports, only horse racing is new to Mario, and it is one of the most fun additions! You get to groom, dress and feed your horses before racing them at top speed against other members of the Mushroom Kingdom.

## FIRM FAVOURITES

The golf and tennis titles use features from two previous games: *Mario Golf: World Tour* (2014) and *Mario Tennis: Ultra Smash* (2015). While gameplay is still good, there's also a feeling that some of the fun factor is missing, with the football for example missing the wild power-ups and over-the-top action we saw in *Mario Strikers Charged* (2007). Still, if you fancy a Mario sports game and are not sure which one you'll enjoy the most, *Mario Sports Superstars* offers a handy taster of each series.

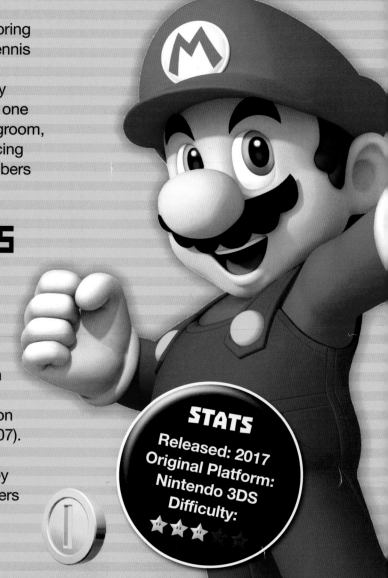

**STATS**
Released: 2017
Original Platform:
Nintendo 3DS
Difficulty:
★★★☆☆

## TRIVIA

Camelot Software Planning have developed all Mario's tennis and golf action since *Mario Golf* (1999) and *Mario Tennis* (2000). They also created Waluigi for *Mario Tennis* when Nintendo wanted a Wario-like rival for Luigi.

## TOP TIP!

If you head out onto the field during horse racing, you can occasionally find a white bird who'll give you a Mario Token. Collect 20 and the final white bird will give you a crate containing the Mario Token Crown, the best accessory you can get for your horse. Well played, your highness!

## SECRET

You can unlock Metal Mario from *Mario 64* (1996) as a team captain if you manage to win the Star Cup. Or if you're feeling lazy, get hold of the Metal Mario amiibo and tap that instead.

# #9

# MARIO TENNIS ACES

Mario's brother can't even pick up a tennis racket without getting possessed by an evil entity in this crazy tennis game. Oh, Luigi!

Adventure Mode in *Mario Tennis Aces* requires Mario to come out on top in a series of tennis-related challenges to turn his bonkers brother back into his normal self again. It just goes to show there can be a lot of love in tennis!

## TENNIS COACH

In actual fact, Adventure Mode is just a clever way to teach you the fun-damentals of the *Mario Tennis* games, so that you become a world-class opponent when you take on up to four friends in the game's multi-player modes. As with all the *Mario Tennis* games, it takes many hours to unlock all the deuce-y characters, and you can be sure that in doing so, you'll make quite a racket. Aces!

## STATS

Released: 2018
Original Platform: Nintendo Switch
Difficulty:
★★★★☆

## TOP TIP!

In the Piranha Plant Court, courtside piranha plants swallow balls and spit them out in different directions so pay attention at all times!

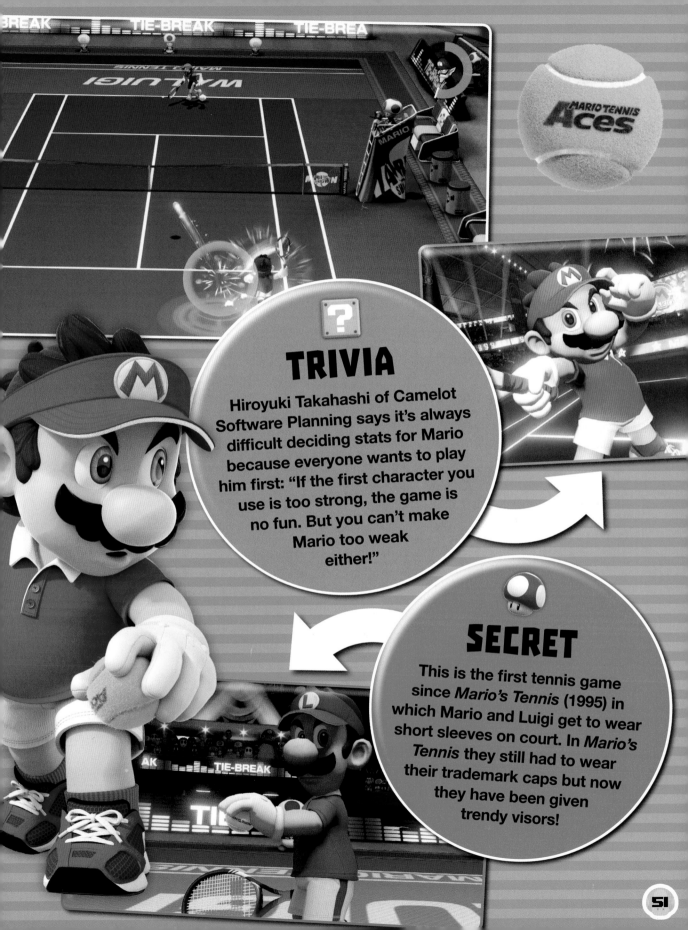

## TRIVIA

Hiroyuki Takahashi of Camelot Software Planning says it's always difficult deciding stats for Mario because everyone wants to play him first: "If the first character you use is too strong, the game is no fun. But you can't make Mario too weak either!"

## SECRET

This is the first tennis game since *Mario's Tennis* (1995) in which Mario and Luigi get to wear short sleeves on court. In *Mario's Tennis* they still had to wear their trademark caps but now they have been given trendy visors!

# FUN GUYS

The Mushroom Kingdom wouldn't really be the Mushroom Kingdom without some toadstools – and these guys are toad-ally the best! Come and meet Mario's favourite mushrooms. They might not look like much but we're sure these fun guys (fungi – geddit?) will grow on you!

## TOAD

| FIRST APPEARANCE: | SUPER MARIO BROS | |
| --- | --- | --- |
| DEBUT YEAR: | | 1985 |
| APPEARANCES: | | 135 |
| STRENGTH: | | 24 |
| SPEED: | | 79 |
| WISDOM: | | 63 |
| COURAGE: | | 71 |

**BIO:** Princess Peach's most loyal servant is almost always by her side. This snappy little dresser is rarely seen without his waistcoat.

## TOADETTE

| FIRST APPEARANCE: | MARIO KART DOUBLE DASH | |
| --- | --- | --- |
| DEBUT YEAR: | | 2003 |
| APPEARANCES: | | 32 |
| STRENGTH: | | 22 |
| SPEED: | | 81 |
| WISDOM: | | 74 |
| COURAGE: | | 65 |

**BIO:** Notable for her interest in music, her cheerful disposition and her bright pink braids, Toadette is firm friends with Toad.

# CAPTAIN TOAD'S TREASURE TRACKER

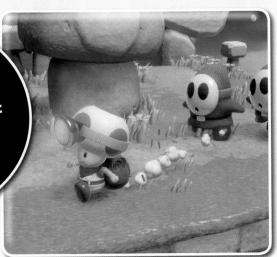

# CAPTAIN TOAD

**FIRST APPEARANCE:**
SUPER MARIO GALAXY
**DEBUT YEAR:** 2013
**APPEARANCES:** 5
**STRENGTH:** 36
**SPEED:** 72
**WISDOM:** 67
**COURAGE:** 54

**BIO:** The leader of the Toad Brigade can be brave but sometimes he's a gigantic coward that makes Luigi look like Mario!

Although the Toads have appeared in hundreds of games, there's only one game where they get a starring and title role. *Captain Toad's Treasure Tracker* is a spin-off of the popular Adventures of Captain Toad levels in *Super Mario 3D World* (2013), which saw our eponymous hero attempting to find treasure in cute isometric puzzle areas. A year later, *Captain Toad's Treasure Tracker* greatly expanded these levels, adding Toadette as a playable character and featuring a proper storyline. It acts as a prequel to *Super Mario 3D World*, with Captain Toad attempting to track down the evil bird that's kidnapped Toadette. It's a fun game with occasional challenges and there are certainly a lot of levels that will leave you scratching your head! An updated version was released for the *Nintendo Switch* in 2018, featuring new levels based on *Super Mario Odyssey*.

# TOADETTE'S PERSONALITY QUIZ

Have you ever wondered which Mario character you're most like? Are you a bold adventurer like Mario, or an evil genius like Bowser? Take this cool quiz to find out!

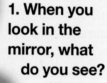

**1. When you look in the mirror, what do you see?**
**a.** It's-a me, Mario!
**b.** Mirrors? There are no mirrors in the lost temples where I spend my days!
**c.** The kindest, prettiest princess in the whole Mushroom Kingdom!
**d.** The cleverest, most handsome king of the Koopas that ever lived! Roar!

**2. You're on Bubblaine Beach and Yoshi asks you to put suncream on him. What do you do?**
**a.** I'm gonna help my best friend!
**b.** I'd love to help but I'm searching for lost treasure! Maybe next time?

**c.** Sorry Yoshi, royalty doesn't really do that kind of thing!
**d.** Suncream? Ha, I'll give you a tan you'll never forget with my flame breath!

**3. Princess Peach has been captured by Bowser again. What do you do?**
**a.** I'm gonna rescue her right away!
**b.** Kidnapped? Is there a reward?
**c.** I'll wait for Mario to arrive, I suppose.
**d.** Kidnapped? Fake News! She wanted to come!

**4. You see a long line of coins. What do you do?**
**a.** I'm gonna collect them all.
**b.** Are they ancient coins from a lost civilisation? No? Not interested.
**c.** I'll ask Toad to gather them up, and keep them safe in the royal treasury.
**d.** Coins? Peach is the only real treasure!

**5. Graffiti has appeared all over Delfino Plaza. There are rumours a certain plumber is responsible. Thoughts?**
a. It's-a not me!
b. It could be ancient clues to hidden treasure!
c. I really do prefer a nice painting!
d. I knew that moustachioed weirdo was too good to be true. Wait, where's Jr.?

**6. You're on Rainbow Road. How do you race your kart?**
a. As-a fast as-a possible, hehe!
b. Karting? I'd rather go tomb-raiding.
c. Actually, I like Toad to drive – carefully.
d. Fast – taking as many shortcuts and throwing as many shells as possible.

**7. Everyone gets hungry from time to time – what's your favourite food?**
a. Mamma mia! It's-a got to be meatballs – with lots-a mushrooms!
b. I'm always on the move – I only eat trail mix!
c. There really is nothing yummier than a freshly baked cake.
d. Yoshi's cookies – stolen fresh from the factory! Rar!

**8. How do you protect yourself during a mission?**
a. All I need is-a two white gloves, two brown shoes, my overalls and a red hat!
b. I always carry a headlamp for dark places, a rope to get me out of tight spots, and a spare pair of shorts in case I… next question?
c. My signature colour – pink!
d. Protection? From who? Mwahaha!

**9. It's important to exercise – what's your favourite sport?**
a. I love golf. It's-a so relaxing!
b. Rock climbing… exploring tombs… running away from monsters!
c. I enjoy a game of tennis occasionally but I'm often too busy to play.
d. Baseball! Any sport where I can hit things really, REALLY hard!

**10. Finally, what's your favourite outfit when you're dressing to impress?**
a. My Tanooki costume – it makes-a me feel like I can fly!
b. My safari suit – light, comfortable, very easy to run away from enemies in!
c. It's hard to choose between the big, puffy, pink dress, the bigger, puffier, pink dress and the biggest, puffiest, pink dress, really!
d. Studded collars… or a wedding suit for Peach!

## RESULTS

**Mostly As:** Were you and Mario separated at birth? You're so similar… and brave!

**Mostly Bs:** You certainly share Captain Toad's bold adventuring spirit! Lead the Brigade!

**Mostly Cs:** You're such a Princess… Peach! Watch out for Bowser types!

**Mostly Ds:** Oh no! You're Bowser's evil twin! What are we going to do with you?

# NEW SUPER MARIO BROS U

When it comes to Mario, Nintendo can get very nostalgic. But let's face it, vintage Mario is quite simply gaming perfection!

After spending years developing the 3D platform game with *Super Mario 64* (1996) and *Super Mario Sunshine* (2002), Nintendo realised that there were still plenty of gamers who missed the charms of the old 2D side-scrolling titles. So, 13 and a half years after *Super Mario Land 2: Six Golden Coins* (1992), it finally released a new 2D game, *New Super Mario Bros.* (2006). But this was no remake – it took the essence of the 2D Mario games and made them fresh, with new levels, and environments but power-ups that still felt like they could have appeared in one of the classic Mario games.

of all time. It was followed by a 3DS sequel, a Wii sequel and most recently, *New Super Mario Bros. U* (2012) for the Wii U, which added Miis and HD graphics into the mix. The story probably won't end there though – you may well be seeing a *New Super Mario Bros. Switch* soon!

## BLAST FROM THE PAST

A monster success on the Nintendo DS, it sold over 30 million copies, making it one of the best-selling games

### STATS

Released: 2012
Original Platform:
Wii U
Difficulty:

★★★★☆

## TRIVIA

2013 was the Year of Luigi, and Nintendo gave the world *New Super Luigi Bros. U* in which Luigi featured as the main character and all the levels were remixed to suit his faster speed and higher jumping abilities.

## TOP TIP!

From *New Super Mario Bros. Wii* (2009) onwards, you can use the Super Guide if you get stuck. Die eight times and a block will appear that will summon Luigi to run the level for you, letting you jump back in at any point. It won't show you any secret coins or hidden exits though!

## SECRET

If you're playing with a pal and run out of lives before they do, you won't be able to play until they complete the level or die. Press the D-pad on your controller for a variety of sound effects that will make them hurry up or distract them to death!

# #7

# MARIO PARTY 10

If you fancy rolling the dice on a new kind of game, why not try out one of the many titles in the *Mario Party* series?

The *Mario Party* games take Snakes and Ladders into a whole new dimension! Mario and friends race across an interactive game board to complete as many mini challenges as possible, before one lucky character (usually a cheating AI player!) is named winner. The first *Mario Party* game appeared back in 1998 on the Nintendo 64 and games like it have appeared on almost every Nintendo console since.

Party Mode, which allows a fifth player to control Bowser using the Wii U GamePad, as the arch villain tries to stop the other players from winning with fireballs and pinball flippers. Well, it's certainly one way to get the party started!

## TWISTED PARTY STARTER

The most recent entry on a home console was *Mario Party 10* (2015) for the Wii U, which re-introduced Donkey Kong as a playable character for the first time since *Mario Party 4* (2006). It also featured Bowser

## SECRET

When it's Bowser's turn during a Bowser Party, wait until he's moving towards the other players and press ^ to hear him unleash a mighty roar!

## STATS

Released: 2015
Original Platform: Wii U
Difficulty:

★

## TRIVIA

The original *Mario Party* left some gamers suffering from 'Analogue Palm' – they got blisters from waggling the joystick back and forth too fast!

## TOP TIP!

The AI players in *Mario Party* games are unbelievably lucky with their dice rolls – always getting exactly the right numbers every time! So, if you can't find enough pals to play with, set the AI players' difficulty to Easy to make things feel fair.

# MARIO & LUIGI SUPERSTAR SAGA

**#6**

If the *Paper Mario* series showcases Mario RPGs on the home consoles, the *Mario & Luigi* series does the same for Mario RPGs on the handheld systems.

Featuring a mix of RPG and action, the *Mario & Luigi* games kicked off with *Mario & Luigi: Superstar Saga* (2003) on the *Gameboy Advance*. Featuring a hilarious script with a cheeky tone (the game opens with Toad walking in on Mario in the shower!), this is the Mushroom Kingdom as you've never seen it before.

saw this series cross over with the *Paper Mario* series, for the ultimate Mario mashup. *Superstar Saga* is arguably the best in the series and Nintendo seem to agree – they re-made it for the 3DS in 2017.

## BROTHERS IN ARMS

There were four sequels in the *Mario & Luigi* series: *Partners in Time* (2005), *Bowser's Inside Story* (2009), *Dream Team* (2013) and *Paper Jam* (2015), which

**STATS**

Released: 2017
Original Platform: Nintendo 3DS
Difficulty:
★★★★☆

## TRIVIA

The 3DS re-make of *Superstar Saga* features a whole new game, *Bowser's Minions*, the story of the first two Goombas you attack. The plot cleverly blends with the main story as you see events from their point of view.

## TOP TIP!

Sometimes it's worth haggling. When you get to the photographer in Beanbean Castle, he'll offer to take your photograph for 100 coins. Say "No" and he'll make a counter offer of 50 coins instead. That ought to put a smile on your face. Now say "Cheese!"

## SECRET

In *Bowser's Minions*, you can find Professor E. Gadd, building the time machine that appears in *Mario & Luigi: Partners in Time!*

# MARIO + RABBIDS: KINGDOM BATTLE

**#5**

You've met the Rabbids, right? Everyone knows those cheeky little bunnies who leave a trail of destruction wherever they go!

Until recently, the Rabbids only caused chaos in the Rayman universe. All that changed when an inventor accidentally sent them to the Mushroom Kingdom in a time-travelling washing machine along with a helmet that could smush things together just by looking at them. *Mario + Rabbids: Kingdom Battle* mashes Mario's world and the Rabbids' kingdom together in a similar way, to create something entirely new for our plumber friend: a turn-based strategy game.

## MIX AND MATCH

Mario, Rabbids and turn-based strategy might sound like a strange combination but in fact *Mario + Rabbids: Kingdom Battle* works very well. Mario is joined by Rabbid versions of his family and friends, such as Rabbid Luigi and Rabbid Peach, as he tries to track down his original family and friends

and free the Mushroom Kingdom from the Rabbid invasion.

**STATS**

Released: 2017
Original Platform: Nintendo Switch
Difficulty:

★★★★☆

## SUPER FUNNY BUNNIES

This is one of the most vibrant Mario games in a very long time. You can tell the Rabbids' creators really enjoyed developing this game from start to finish. Every world is packed full of humour and fun references to previous Mario games – there's even a mini Mario opera tucked away in there! If you fancy playing a Mario game that's had a lot of thought (and even more giggles) put into it, then you should definitely give this one a go.

## TRIVIA

Nintendo loves collaboration but *Mario + Rabbids: Kingdom Battle* was the first time they let a European developer – Ubisoft – get involved with Mario.

## TOP TIP!

In World 1's first challenge, use Rabbid Mario (with Golden Shot and Magnet Dance) to attract and beat enemies with his Magnet, Hammer and Red Lightning. Peach (with Golden Shot Plus Level 2) has a Blue Flame to help him. Beating them all will win you 215 gold coins!

## SECRET

When you recruit Rabbid Yoshi, check out his grenades. One is a Grenaduck called Sam Kingfisher – a sneaky nod to Sam Fisher, the star of Ubisoft's *Splinter Cell* games.

# BLOCK PARTY

The question mark block is the first block you come across in *Super Mario Bros.* (1985) and it's filled with possibilities. Could it contain a coin, a mushroom or something even more exotic? Don't get too excited... it'll probably be a coin!

## ! BLOCK

The ! block first appeared in *Super Mario World* (1990) as a series of dotted lines, only becoming a solid block when the correct colour switch had been activated in a nearby switch palace. They often contain power-ups and extra lives.

## POW BLOCK

The oldest block, the POW block first appeared back in 1983 in *Mario Bros.* It has cropped up in most of the games since then, causing an enemy-destroying earthquake when jumped on, thrown or punched.

## NOTE BLOCK

Note blocks have appeared in almost every Mario platform game since *Super Mario Bros. 3*, and if you press the jump button just as you land on one, it will act as a springboard, sending you higher than you'd ever thought possible!

## COIN BLOCK

If you want to make it rain, coin blocks can be hit multiple times to release a fountain of coins into the air. Hit it 10 times quickly enough, and in some Mario games you may sometimes get an extra bonus.

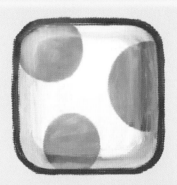

## EGG BLOCK

Only seen in Yoshi games such as *Yoshi's Story* (1997) and *Yoshi's New Island* (2014), these boxes store eggs for Yoshi to use as ammunition. They can be recognized by their colourful exterior, square shape, and yucky smell!

# #4

# SUPER MARIO RUN

Although he's no stranger to handheld devices, *Mario Run* gave the moustachioed hero his first adventure inside a mobile phone.

For Mario's phone debut, Nintendo went for a classic side-scrolling runner game. It's closest in style to the *New Super Mario Bros.* titles, but with one important twist: this time, you don't get to control Mario's movement, only his jumps. You'd think that this would make the game far too simple to play but in typical Nintendo style there's a lot of depth hidden amongst the easy mechanics. Tapping the screen mid-jump will see you do a spin, and tapping while next to a wall will make Mario do a wall jump in the opposite direction.

## APP-EALING GAMEPLAY

With multiple paths through them, the levels are designed to be played more than once. You'll need to finish each level at least three times to collect

the special pink, purple and black coins that have been hidden in hard-to-reach places. You can spend any coins you collect on new buildings and playable characters. There's plenty of fantastic gaming packed into this little app. If you're ready for some Mario action on the go – and especially if you've only got one hand free! – this is the perfect choice for you.

**STATS**

Released: 2017
Original Platform:
iOS/Android
Difficulty:

⭐⭐☆☆☆

**SECRET**

If you have an iPhone, you might find you're not the only Mario fan in the house. Try telling Siri: "It's Mario Time!" and see what she says…

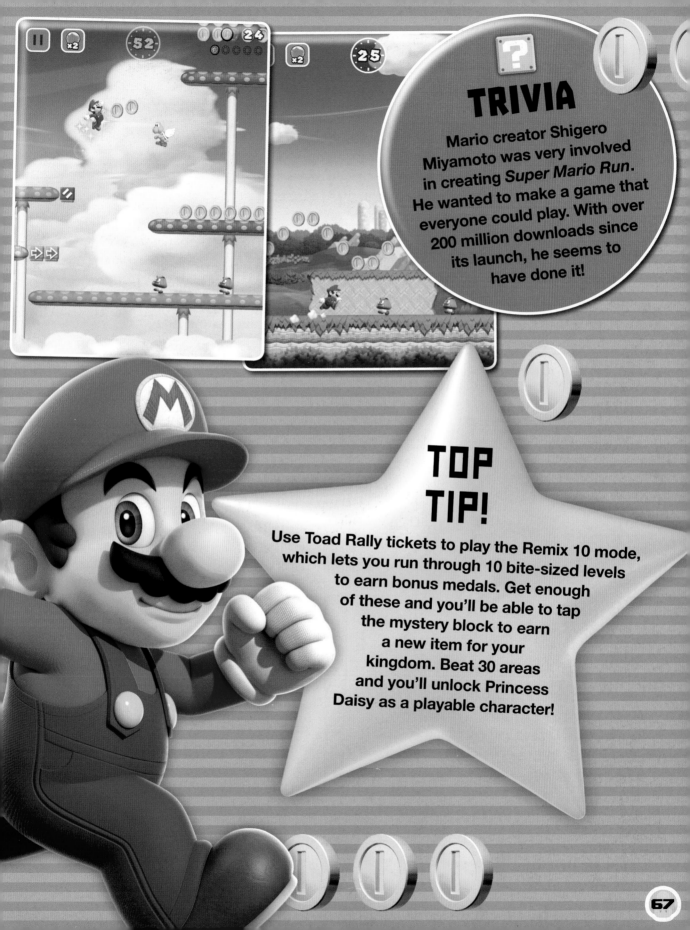

## TRIVIA

Mario creator Shigero Miyamoto was very involved in creating *Super Mario Run*. He wanted to make a game that everyone could play. With over 200 million downloads since its launch, he seems to have done it!

## TOP TIP!

Use Toad Rally tickets to play the Remix 10 mode, which lets you run through 10 bite-sized levels to earn bonus medals. Get enough of these and you'll be able to tap the mystery block to earn a new item for your kingdom. Beat 30 areas and you'll unlock Princess Daisy as a playable character!

# WARIO'S WICKED QUIZ

This quiz about Mario is so difficult it'll melt your brain! Think you've got what it takes to win? Well, think again!

## WARIO

**FIRST APPEARANCE:** SUPER MARIO LAND 2: SIX GOLDEN COINS

**DEBUT YEAR:** 2013

**APPEARANCES:** 103

**STRENGTH:** 89

**SPEED:** 77

**WISDOM:** 86

**COURAGE:** 71

**BIO:** With his wild moustache and ketchup-covered overalls, Mario's dark twin loves garlic almost as much as himself!

**1. What year was the first Mario game released?**
a. 1981
b. 1066
c. 1985
d. Don't know...

**2. Mario and Luigi are brothers. But what's their surname?**
a. Romano
b. Mario
c. Johnson
d. How should I know?

**3. Which was the first game that Mario spoke in?**
a. Super Mario 64
b. Super Mario World
c. Mario's Game Gallery

**d.** How old was he when he first spoke? In his thirties? His parents must have been so proud!

**4. Princess Peach is a good name. But what name did she use in her earliest games?**
    **a.** Princess Toadstool
    **b.** Princess Buttercup
    **c.** Princess Ramsbottom
    **d.** It doesn't matter, she'll always be pretty as a Peach to me!

**5. Love? It's-a pain! But who was Mario's first girlfriend?**
    **a.** Princess Daisy
    **b.** Princess Peach
    **c.** Pauline
    **d.** As if he ever had a girlfriend!

**6. Where did Mario meet his pet Yoshi?**
**a.** Delfino Island
**b.** Dinosaur Island
**c.** Monster Island
**d.** A pet store… a terrible one!

**7. Which famous Japanese game designer was responsible for creating Mario?**
**a.** Yu Suzuki
**b.** Vincent Van Gough
**c.** Shigeru Miyamoto
**d.** It was Wario, the greatest game designer ever!

**8. How many games has Mario appeared in?**
**a.** 234

**b.** 153
**c.** 689
**d.** How many? Why isn't Wario in more?

**9. Mario's Tanooki Suit makes him look like a raccoon! Which game did it first appear in?**
**a.** *Super Mario 3D World*
**b.** *Mario Paint*
**c.** *Super Mario Bros. 3*
**d.** Doesn't matter! Wario always looks better!

**10. Finally, the most important question: How did Wario get his name?**
**a.** It's Mario with the M upside down.
**b.** It's a combination of the Japanese word for 'evil' and Mario.
**c.** Wario is Japanese for 'bad plumber.'
**d.** His mum thought Wario was simply the greatest name ever!

# RESULTS

**So how many of Wario's super-clever questions did you get right?**
**1-3:** Oh no! You didn't stand a chance against his tricky test! Wario wins again!
**4-6:** Hmmm, you know a few things but you're no expert. Maybe you need to pay a bit more attention to Wario, and Mario!
**7-9:** What? That's incredible! Next time, Wario will have to make the questions much harder, just for you!
**10:** You're a genius! Are you sure you're not a plumber in disguise?

# SUPER MARIO MAKER

**#3**

Over the years, you've probably played hundreds of brilliant levels, but wouldn't you love to create some of your very own?

*Super Mario Maker* lets you create Mario levels to your heart's content. As well as including sounds, graphics and levels from every Mario era, it features a toy box that's brimming with Super Mario Building Blocks. You can build everything from a super old-school, NES-style level to something more modern such as *New Super Mario Bros.* You can even share your creations with other players on the internet.

## STATS

Released: 2015
Original Platform:
Wii U/3DS
Difficulty:

★

increase the challenge. A Mushroom will also make cloud-surfing Lakitu throw Koopas at the player. If you feel like setting your creative side free there's no better teacher than Mario. The only limit with this game is your imagination!

## LIMITLESS POSSIBILITIES

Creating levels using the Wii U or 3DS stylus is incredibly easy, but the true joy is how the editor allows you to combine elements to create whole new experiences. For example, you can drag a Mushroom onto enemies to make them bigger and

## TRIVIA

Ideas never get thrown away at Nintendo, they are just filed away until they're ready for the spotlight... the thinking behind *Super Mario Maker* began way back in 1994 when Nintendo filed a patent for video game hardware that let players pause a game and re-edit the level.

# TOP TIP!

Don't forget to shake and tap everything with your stylus. You'll find hidden animations, funny sounds or if you use it to knock on doors, you may meet some special guests!

# SECRET

*Super Mario Maker* is stuffed with secrets – try tapping the logo letters on the title screen with your stylus! Our favourite is this hidden minigame Gnat Attack. Grab a Muncher and shake it until three Gnats appear. Tap all three to start the game. Complete it to unlock a new costume for Mario!

# #2

# SUPER SMASH BROS. FOR WII U / 3DS

**Have you ever wanted to see Mario really show Kirby who's boss? Then *Super Smash Bros.* is the series for you!**

A royal rumble of video game characters, these games let you finally settle all those playground arguments over whether Sonic the Hedgehog could beat Mario in a fight. The brilliance of *Smash Bros.* is that, unlike most fighting games, every character essentially uses the same buttons, so you don't have to learn endless lists of button combinations when you switch to a new character. Instead of health bars, each character has a damage meter – the more damage you take, the higher the meter gets, and the more likely it is that your character will get smashed off the stage.

Nintendo favourites such as Mario, Bowser, Link and various Pokémon are present, but you can also expect to smash into Mega Man, Pac-Man and Bayonetta during your four- or eight-player brawls. With its numerous game modes and competitive online scene, this really is an awesome package. And watch out for the upcoming *Super Smash Bros. Switch* – Nintendo are set to smash it out of the park with this new game.

# MASSIVE GUEST LIST

## STATS

Released: 2014
Original Platform: Wii U/3DS
Difficulty:

*Super Smash Bros.* for Wii U is the latest entry, and it features no less than 58 characters. All your

## TRIVIA

*Super Smash Bros.* was based on a secret demo by Masahiro Sukurai (a producer at HAL Laboratories) featuring Mario, Donkey Kong, Metroid's Samus and Starfox's Fox McCloud.

## SECRET

When you're playing a coin battle, take a closer look at one of the dollar bills. You see that nondescript building? It's the Nintendo headquarters, situated in Kyoto, Japan!

## TOP TIP!

One of the best characters to learn when you're first starting out is Mario! He's got a decent range attack with his fireballs, and his F.L.U.D.D. device from *Mario Sunshine* can really punish rivals as they try to recover from a beating. Easily one of the most versatile characters in the game, Mario can dish out a beating quicker than you can say, "Mamma mia!"

# MARIO'S MOST WANTED

Over the years, Mario has punished hundreds of baddies in the Mushroom Kingdom but they just keep coming back. Here's a guide to the worst ones!

## KOOPA TROOPA

**First Appearance:**
*Super Mario Bros.* (1985)

Koopa Troopas are the loyal foot soldiers of the Koopa Troop, experts in obstruction and firing shells at the enemy. They come in many colours. Blue shells are the clingy ones. You don't like them? They're turtle-y fine with that!

## SHY GUY

**First Appearance:**
*Super Mario Bros. 2* (1988)

Shy Guys certainly live up to their name – they hide their faces behind masks at all times. Even Bowser doesn't know what they really look like. When they're not causing mischief for Mario, they enjoy dance-offs and practising their circus skills.

# LAKITU

**First Appearance:**
*Super Mario Bros.*
(1985)

Lakitu spends
his time floating
around in the sky,
sometimes hurling
Spineys at passers-by and telling them
to get off of his cloud. He also likes
film-making and filmed all of Mario's
adventures in *Super Mario 64*.

# THWOMP

**First Appearance:**
*Super Mario Bros. 3*
(1988)

Made from
the living rock
of the Mushroom Kingdom, Thwomps
like nothing more than squashing
things, and on the rare occasions
they get invited to parties, they spend
most of their time in the kitchen
crushing cans against their heads.

# BULLET BILL

**First
Appearance:**
*Super Mario
Bros.* (1985)

There aren't many guns in the
Mushroom Kingdom but there are
plenty of bullets! Fired from Bullet
Blasters, these serious little chaps
follow Mario everywhere, tracking
him with laser-guided precision.

# GOOMBA

**First Appearance:**
*Super Mario Bros.*
(1985)

Goombas may be weak but there's
strength in numbers and there
certainly are a lot of them. Before
they joined Bowser's Koopa Troop,
Goombas used to be peaceful
creatures… maybe one day, they
will be peace-loving again.

# BOO

**First Appearance:**
*Super Mario Bros. 3*
(1988)

Boos love to hide in dark, spooky
places, like haunted mansions,
castles, or race tracks. They
are almost impossible to look at
directly but they are also extremely
vulnerable to vacuum cleaners.

# #1

# SUPER MARIO ODYSSEY

**Mario has been from Brooklyn to the centre of the universe, and everywhere in between, but *Odyssey* might be his craziest trip yet!**

Bowser and Princess Peach are getting married and this time Bowser is really pulling out all the stops. He's grabbing her the Soirée Bouquet from the Wooded Kingdom, getting a wedding dress from the Lake Kingdom and planning a ceremony on the moon. The only problem is, Peach doesn't actually want to marry him. After Bowser kidnaps his beloved but still unwilling bride, it's up to Mario to run after Bowser and rescue Peach once again. Luckily, he's not alone, as a young Bonneter named Cappy has replaced his trademark cap. Cappy gives Mario the ability to possess enemies, items and even T Rexes, who all naturally sport his fabulous moustache while they're under his spell!

## STATS
Released: 2017
Original Platform:
Nintendo Switch
Difficulty:
★★★☆☆

*Sunshine* (2002), and each kingdom Mario visits is stuffed with things to do and Power Moons to collect. Almost every era of Mario is represented here, from 2D side-scrolling levels, to special guest appearances from Yoshi and Luigi. If you only take on one epic Super Mario adventure, choose *Odyssey*!

## IT'S-A EPIC!

*Super Mario Odyssey* represents a return to the sandbox-style of *Super Mario*

## TRIVIA

One game that had a big impact on the development of *Super Mario Odyssey* was *Minecraft*. Watching *Minecraft* videos on YouTube convinced Kenta Motokura, the director of *Super Mario Odyssey*, that having to manipulate the camera in the game wouldn't make it too difficult for modern kids to play.

## TOP TIP!

In this Seaside Kingdom mini-game, there's an easy way to return the ball 100 times and get a Power Moon. Turn on two player mode, activate the challenge with Mario, step off the court, launch Cappy and use the second controller to reach the balls much more quickly. That Power Moon will soon be yours!

## SECRET

New Donk City is a tribute to *Donkey Kong* (1981), the game that started it all for Mario. Mayor Pauline (below) was Donkey Kong's first kidnap victim and the focus of Mario's first rescue attempt. She even refers to it in the quiz she gives Mario in *Odyssey*.

## SCOOTER BOOST

One of the hardest Power Moons in the game to get is definitely the skipping rope challenge in New Donk City. The first Power Moon is easy enough to achieve – just jump over the twirling rope 30 times. The second one requires you to do it 100 times in a row though, which can feel almost impossible. But get on a scooter (which has a much more reliable jumping pattern), and you should be able to do it with ease.

## GO FOR GOLD!

You'll need to collect Power Moons to power up the Odyssey (your hat-shaped ship), and you'll only need to collect around half of the available Moons to see the game's first ending. But if you really want a challenge, why not try to collect all 999? If you do, you'll get a fancy gold balloon and a fireworks display back at Peach's Castle!

# TOP TIP!

*Super Mario Odyssey* isn't a very difficult game to finish but if you're finding it tough (or if you want to take on the tougher levels after beating the game), then simply turn on Assist Mode in the main menu. It not only doubles your health, but it also rescues you if you fall off a ledge, which will definitely help you keep your cool on some of the ridiculously long levels at the end of the game.

# SECRET

You knew that Mario was a massive fashion icon, didn't you? The costumes in *Super Mario Odyssey* are borrowed from a host of previous Mario games. See if you can spot the Doctor Mario costume, the Mario chef outfit from *Yoshi's Cookies* (1992), the golf outfit from *NES Open Tournament Golf* (1991) and the awesome *Super Mario 64* outfit, complete with Nintendo 64-era pointy polygons!

# THAT'S-A ALL FOLKS!

That's the end of the book! Now it's time to pick up your phone or controller and get playing!